Ancient Egypt

Written by
Diane Sylvester

Illustrated by
Corbin Hillam

2 0 0 6 • T H E   L E A R N I N G   W O R K S

The Learning Works

Editor: Pam VanBlaricum
Illustrator: Corbin Hillam
Text Design: Acorn Studio Books
Cover Designer: Barbara Peterson
Cover Illustration: Gary Ciccarelli
Project Director: Linda Schwartz

Contents

◥•◤

To the Teacher

Purpose

Museums are storehouses of interesting things that help us learn more about our natural and physical world. The purpose of this book is to provide ideas and activities to help students create their own amazing museum full of specially crafted artifacts from the ancient civilization of Egypt.

The projects and activities in this book highlight the economic, political, social, scientific, and cultural components upon which all civilizations are based.

The projects and activities also provide these opportunities for students:

- Plan and give oral presentations

- Plan and conduct guided tours

- Plan and create graphs, labels, and posters

- Refine map reading skills

Social Studies Standards

The content of this book will allow the learner to meet the following social studies standards:

Analyze the geographic, political, religious, and social structures of ancient Egypt.

Locate and describe the Nile river system and discuss the physical settings that supported permanent settlement and early civilizations.

Understand the relationship between religion and the social and political order in Egypt.

Discuss the main features of Egyptian art and architecture.

Understand the significance of Queen Hatsheput and Ramses the Great.

Trace the evolution of language and its written forms.

Understand the contributions of ancient Egypt.

Demonstrate knowledge of what archaeological evidence indicates.

Tips and Ideas for Setting up the Ancient Egypt Museum

Creating a museum is often used as a culmination to a unit of study. However, creating a museum can be a unit by itself—full of educational and motivational activities and projects. The following ideas will help you and your students set up your ancient civilization museum.

Decisions to make before you begin

Where will the museum be located?

What roles will students assume in creating the artifacts and in displaying them?

How many artifacts will be included in the museum?

How will the students be grouped for each activity (individual, small group, or entire class)?

Suggestions for student roles

(The teacher should decide whether or not to assume the roles of Museum Director and/or Curator)

Museum Director: this person assigns roles and coordinates lessons and activities

Curator: this person chooses the artifacts to be constructed and displayed; oversees placement of artifacts in museum; oversees labeling and educational material accompanying artifact

Design and Planning Specialists: students, or small groups of students, plan, make, and display artifacts

Public Education Advisors: students write scripts for tours; oversee training tour guides; and create advertising or educational videos

Advertisers: students create brochures, posters, advertisements, and invitations

Reporters: students write articles for class newspaper or other school publications

Tour Guides: students lead parents and other students on tour of museum

Tips and Ideas for Setting Up
the Ancient Egypt Museum *(continued)*

Suggestions for planning and creating your museum

Give your museum a creative name.

Make a large map of Egypt.

Make a mural highlighting important achievements in ancient Egyptian history.

Consider making artifacts in a variety of ways—drawn, sculpted, carved, modeled, sewn, photographed, etc.

Consider using a variety of materials for the artifacts such as clay, papier mache, cardboard, wood, yarn, foil, etc.

The exhibit displays can be set on stands, put in boxes, hung from ceilings, attached to walls, placed on floors, etc.

Make signs for museum—posters, bulletin boards, display stands, etc.

Publicize exhibit by creating pamphlets, posters, brochures, advertisements, videos, etc.

Create tour brochures, tour guide speeches, and audio tours.

Invite other classes and parents to grand opening of museum.

The Grand Opening of the museum can begin with an ancient Egyptian funeral procession. Students can play drums, bells, or recorders, or they can clap. In addition, students can dress appropriately to represent people from pharaohs to gods or goddesses. At the end of the procession, the mummy, canopic jars, and other artifacts can be placed in a tomb designed by students.

As part of the opening ceremonies, a special celebration can be held. Think of a name for the event such as An Evening at the Pharaoh's or The Pharaoh's Nile Tour. Some components of the celebration can be costumes, food, music, and individual presentations.

     Ancient Egypt © 2006 The Learning Works

Invitation to the Grand Opening
of the Ancient Egypt Museum

cut here

Celebrate the Grand Opening of the

⇒ Ancient Egypt Museum ⇐

Date: _____   Time: _____

Location: _____

_____

Organized and Created by

_____

_____

_____

Exhibits • Displays • Ancient Artifacts • Personal Tours

Exhibit Description Card

Directions

Photocopy exhibit cards on heavyweight paper. Make one card per exhibit. Complete the information, fold the card, and place it alongside the museum artifact.

fold here

⋙ Ancient Egypt Museum ⋘

Name of artifact: _____

Description: _____

_____

_____

_____

Designed and created by _____

cut here

Ancient Egypt Project Proposal

Directions

Submit a completed *Ancient Egypt Project Proposal* to your museum director or curator for approval.

Name(s): _____

Title of artifact/project: _____

Description of artifact/project: _____

_____

_____

What materials will you need? _____

_____

_____

How much room in the museum will your project need? _____

Write a short script describing the artifact/project for a museum tour guide to use.

_____

_____

_____

_____

Brochure for Grand Opening
of the Ancient Egypt Museum

Directions

Design a brochure or flyer that describes the exhibits in your museum. You may use the clip art on this page or draw your own illustrations.

Ancient Egypt © 2006 The Learning Works

Techniques for Creating Artifacts

Papier Mache Projects

Papier mache projects are easy to make—basically layering of paper over a shape—but can be messy and take several days to dry. Instant papier mache products are available from craft stores.

Materials

Pulp: Newspaper is a key ingredient for the papier mache pulp. Newspaper can also be used for creating details such as appendages, decorations, or facial features. Other types of papers can be used too, such as paper towels, tissue paper, and toilet paper. Some people recommend using brown paper bags because they are cleaner to use. Interesting effects can be achieved with fancy wrapping papers.

Paste: There are many different recipes for papier mache paste. Two of the easiest are ordinary liquid starch or a mixture of one part water with two parts white glue.

Shaped forms:
You can create forms (armature or skeleton) for your papier mache projects
from these suggested items:
   toilet paper and paper towel rolls
   egg cartons
   balloons (pop when papier mache is dry)
   aluminum pie pans
   paper cups
   cardboard boxes such as cereal boxes, oatmeal containers,
      and shoe boxes
   crumpled or rolled newspapers
   crunched aluminum foil

Other materials:
   masking tape for holding the form components together
   bowl for paste
   scissors
   brushes to brush on paste, if preferred
   tempera or poster paints
   decorating items such as crepe paper, ribbons, glitter,
      beads, yarn, gold foil, old jewelry, etc.

Techniques for Creating Artifacts *(continued)*

Directions

1. Design the artifact on paper and then create the form out of suggested materials.

2. Tear or cut paper into strips.

3. Pour paste into a bowl. Dip each strip into the paste a few seconds, but don't soak it.

4. Place the strip where you want it on the form and smooth it down. Let the first layer dry thoroughly before adding another layer. It will also work to apply three or four layers before letting it dry, especially if time is short.

5. Use crushed or rolled newspaper to make appendages or other attachments. Use masking tape to attach these to the form. Papier mache the attachments.

6. Use pieces of newspaper to thicken features, or use wadded up paper pulp to form features.

7. Apply a final layer of white paper (paper towels, white tissue paper) so that the paint goes on easier. Use brown paper toweling for a different effect.

8. Let the artifact dry completely, and then paint it.

9. When the paint has dried, decorate the artifact with decorative items, if desired.

   Ancient Egypt © 2006 The Learning Works

Techniques for Creating Artifacts *(continued)*

Clay Projects

Clay can be manipulated into many shapes and designs and is a perfect medium for making ancient civilization artifacts. Try to find clay that doesn't require baking or firing to save time and to make the process easier.

Materials

> modeling clay or clay and sculpting materials that don't require firing or baking. Several types will dry bone hard and can be decorated, painted, and modified by sanding or filing.
> tools for sculpting
> toothpicks
> paring knife or utility blade
> coffee stirrers
> cuticle sticks
> textures from fabrics, window screen, sandpaper, emery boards, etc.
> plastic forks and knives
> craft sticks
> grater for making hair
> rolling pin for brayer

Directions

1. Decide on the size and type of artifact you will sculpt. You'll probably need 1–2 pounds of clay for each large artifact. Store extra clay in a sealable plastic bag or in a container with a lid. With air-dry clay, it is important to cover it with a wet cloth when not working on it.

2. Keep your sculpture on a piece of board or thick paper while working on it. Use the pinch method to anchor the feet to the base. Make it solid for stability.

3. Begin by rolling or forming clay to create the main part of the artifact.

4. Make appendages by rolling clay into a ball or rolling out "worms." Push a piece of clay through a cheese grater to make hair or other features.

5. Add details by using some of the tools suggested above.

6. Keep your figure in its original clay color, or paint it in realistic colors.

Techniques for Creating Artifacts *(continued)*

Foil Projects

Foil works well for making artifacts because it is easy to create a good basic shape. It has volume and can be worked and reworked until you get the shape you want.

Materials

    aluminum foil
    permanent ink marking pens
    masking tape
    paint
    cardboard
    scissors
    glue

Directions

1. On a sheet of paper, make a plan that details the components of the project.

2. Use foil to create the objects in your project. Gently crumple foil together. If you squeeze too hard, the foil compresses and the person or animal gets too thin.

3. Use extra pieces of foil to strengthen arms and legs or parts of the model.

4. Take the masking tape and completely cover each person or animal model.

5. A thin layer of papier mache can be applied over the model and the masking tape. Otherwise, paint over the masking tape and draw in authentic details.

Ancient Egypt © 2006 The Learning Works

Ancient Egypt: A Land of Contrasts

Egypt was the birthplace of one of the world's first civilizations. The center of the Egyptian civilization was the Nile River, the longest river in the world. The ancient Egyptians thought of Egypt as being divided into two types of land—the "black land" referring to the fertile, black silt along the Nile, and the "red land" referring to the desolate desert area which protected Egypt from neighboring countries and invading armies.

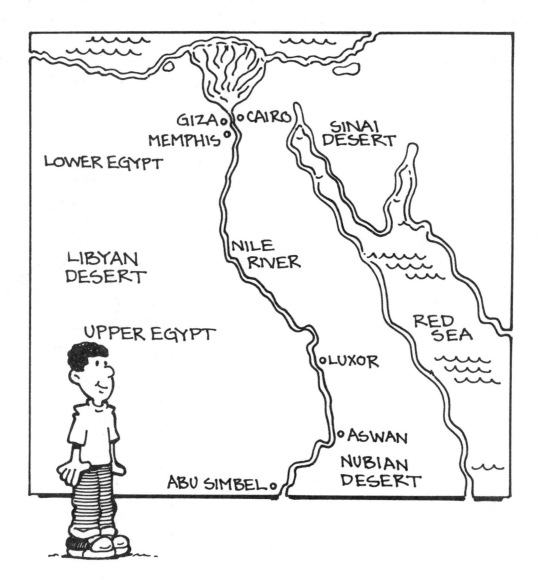

Project Description

Make a relief map of ancient Egypt out of papier mache (pages 12–13). The map should include the Nile River, Giza, Memphis, Cairo, the Nile Delta, the Red Sea, the Nubian Desert, Abu Simbel, Aswan, Luxor, and other places pertinent to the artifacts in the museum. Display the map in a prominent location such as near the entrance to the museum.

Timeline of Ancient Egyptian History

Ancient Egypt's history spanned 3,000 years and at least thirty dynasties or ruling families. Ancient Egyptian dynasties are grouped into periods called "kingdoms." Exact dates of dynasties are not always known precisely.

The ancient Egyptians made outstanding contributions to world history. They created the world's first national government and a calendar that divided the year into 365 days. They invented a form of picture writing using hieroglyphs. They also invented papyrus, a writing material made from papyrus plants. They developed one of the first religions to emphasize life after death and built great cities in which many skilled architects, doctors, engineers, painters, and sculptors worked. Mostly, though, the ancient Egyptians are famous for the pyramids they built as tombs for their rulers.

Some Important Egyptian Dynasties

Among the many problems encountered in Egyptology, one of the most controversial is that of dating events. The kingdom dates are approximate and based on the Theban Mapping Project, American University, Cairo, Egypt.

Early Dynastic Period, ca. 3100–2700 B.C.
Menes, 3100–2850 B.C.

Old Kingdom, 2700–2184 B.C.
Djoser, 2630–2611 B.C.
Khufu (Cheops), 2551–2528 B.C.
Khafra, 2520–2494 B.C.

Middle Kingdom, 2040–1782 B.C.
Senwosret III, 1836–1817 B.C.
Amenemhat III, 1817–1772 B.C.

New Kingdom, 1570–1070 B.C.
Hatshepsut, 1504–1458 B.C.
Akhenaten or Amenhotep IV, 1350–1334 B.C.
Tutankhamen, 1334 or 1333–1323 B.C.
Rameses II, 1290–1224 B.C.

Project Description

When you write the description card for the items that will be in your museum, try to identify the dynasty in which it was invented, built, or gained popularity.

The Pharaohs' Crowns

At one point in ancient times, Egypt was two kingdoms—Lower Egypt (land downstream or to the north) and Upper Egypt (land upstream or to the south). The kings of Upper Egypt wore a white crown, while the kings of Lower Egypt wore a red crown. For centuries the two kingdoms fought each other to gain control of the whole region. Menes was the first king to unify Upper and Lower Egypt into one kingdom. After unification, the Egyptian pharaohs began to wear a crown that was a combination of the crowns of both kingdoms. Each crown had a serpent, or snake, at the front that was the symbol of royalty. (Some Egyptologists think that the pharaoh Narmer unified Egypt; some hold that Narmer and Menes are the same person; still others hold that Menes completed a process of unification started by Narmer.)

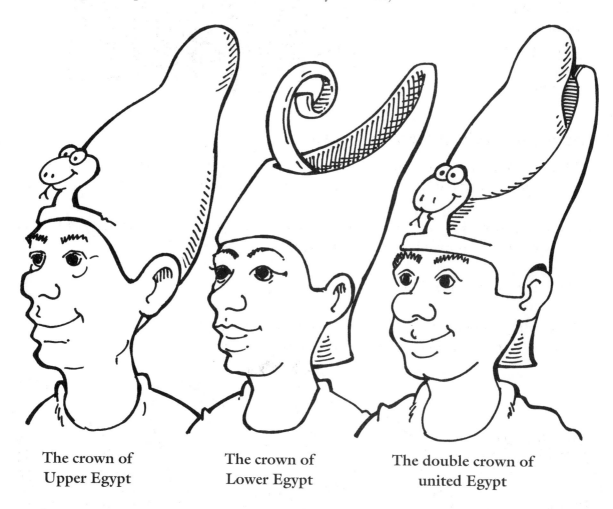

| The crown of Upper Egypt | The crown of Lower Egypt | The double crown of united Egypt |

Project Description

Several renowned Egyptologists will be attending the grand opening of the Ancient Egypt Museum. You and your staff want to impress them with your knowledge of Menes and the unification of Upper and Lower Egypt. Study art work showing historical depictions of the crowns, and then re-create one of them for the museum.

The Pharaohs' Crowns *(continued)*

Materials

cardboard or poster board
foil
newspaper
felt
masking tape
string
white glue or liquid starch
white tempera paint
brushes
marking pens
stapler
gold foil

Directions for making the white crown

1. Measure a four-inch-wide strip of cardboard so that it fits around your head. Staple the ends together. Cut out the ear openings. This is the foundation of the crown.

2. Use newspaper or foil to build the bowling-pin-shaped crown. Use masking tape to anchor the newspaper to the cardboard strip. Then papier mache the form.

3. When the papier mache is dry, paint it white.

4. Make a serpent out of foil, cover it in masking tape, and papier mache it. Use marking pens to add features. Glue the serpent to the front of the crown.

The Pharaohs' Crowns (continued)

Directions for making the red crown

1. Draw a pattern of the crown on a piece of poster board. Make sure the crown will fit on your head. (You can measure your head with a piece of string and use that as a guide for your head circumference measurement. Make the crown a couple of inches wider so it can be glued or stapled together.)

2. Cut out the crown, making sure that the spot for connecting the crown is at the side of the crown and not the back. Paint the poster board or glue red felt onto it.

3. Staple the crown together. Make a serpent out of cardboard, cardboard and felt, or gold foil. Attach it to the crown.

4. For the unified crown, the white and red crowns can be combined and worn together.

Egyptian Scrolls

Hieroglyphs, the characters in the ancient Egyptian writing system, were carved on monuments, pyramids, and tombs, or written in ink on papyrus scrolls. Hieroglyphs used pictures to represent different words, actions, or ideas. Some pictures stood for whole words; others simply stood for a sound and were joined with other signs to make a word.

Although vowels were used in the spoken language, they were not usually written out. For example, we might write "blg" when we would say "building" or "mtn" for "mountain." Hiero-glyphic writing was written in columns or rows. The direction that the figures faced determined the reading direction, either from left to right or from right to left.

Scribes were the few Egyptians who knew how to read and write. Young scribes—almost always boys from wealthy or royal families—would attend school for years to become adept at writing and reading.

Egyptian Scrolls *(continued)*

Project Description

The museum curator of the Ancient Egypt Museum put a great deal of time, money, and effort into setting up new museum exhibits. However, one important exhibit is incomplete. The curator knows that Egyptian books consisted of scrolls, which were long pieces of rolled papyrus, and that libraries existed in ancient Egypt, some housing 100,000 or more scrolls. The curator wants to create a library in the museum and has assigned you the task of making models of scrolls. You may create your own story, poem, or message, but it must be done in hieroglyphs with appropriate Egyptian drawings.

Materials

parchment paper, brown paper bag, or other
    paper that resembles papyrus paper
tea bag to make paper look old (optional)
marking pens
acrylic paints, including black and gold
glue
raffia

Directions

1. Glue paper sheets together to create a scroll about 22 inches long, or creat a shorter scroll fragment.

2. Antique the paper by gently rubbing a damp tea bag over it.

3. Research actual Egyptian scrolls, and then make a sketch of what your scroll, or scroll fragment, will look like.

4. Use colored marking pens, or acrylic paints, for the hieroglyphs, drawings, and designs.

5. When the scroll is completely dry, roll it up and tie it with a piece of raffia.

     Ancient Egypt © 2006 The Learning Works

Royal Cartouches

A cartouche is an oval or oblong shape containing the hieroglyphic name of an ancient Egyptian pharaoh, queen, or other high-ranking person.

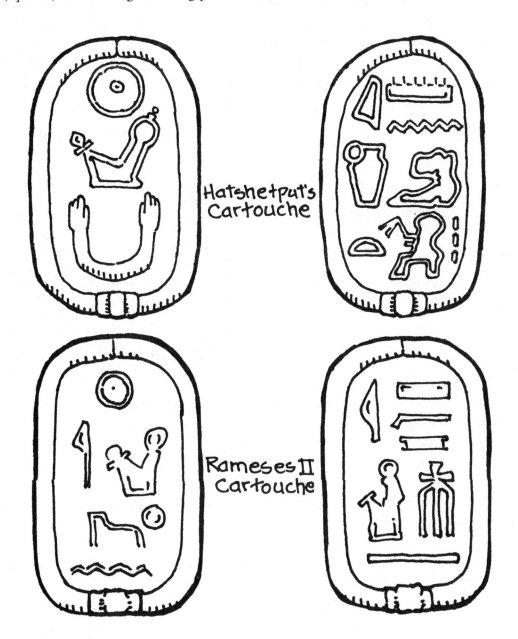

Hatshetput's Cartouche

Rameses II Cartouche

Project Description

Your archaeological expedition reached one of the halls located outside a pharaoh's burial chamber. The carvings, statues, and cartouches found in this area are amazing. It inspires you to ask your museum staff to create cartouches using their own names written in hieroglyphs. Make the cartouches out of clay and place them in your Ancient Egypt Museum.

Royal Cartouches *(continued)*

Materials

    clay or sculpting materials that
        don't require firing or baking
    rolling pin or brayer
    carving tools
    plastic knife or other tool for cutting out the cartouche
    gold paint or spray
    black marking pen or black ink
    shoebox lid or heavy cardboard

Directions

1. Roll out clay using a rolling pin, brayer, or other round object, to about 1/2 inch thick.

2. Cut out the base of the cartouche. It should measure about four inches wide and twelve inches long. (While you are working on the cartouche, store it in the shoebox lid or on cardboard covered with plastic.)

3. Use the hieroglyphics chart on page 21 to translate your name into hieroglyphs.

4. Carve the hieroglyphs into the clay.

5. Roll out long rope-like pieces of clay to be used around the edges and at the bottom of the cartouche. Blend them into the base leaving a rim.

6. Some cartouches have a knotted rope design at the bottom of the cartouche. Use a thicker rope-like piece of clay for this addition. Shape it carefully with your fingers or with sculpting tools.

7. When your cartouche is completely dry, paint or spray paint it gold. Then fill in each hieroglyph with black ink or a black marking pen.

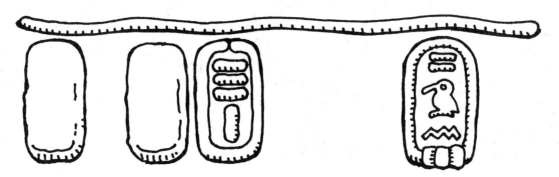

       Ancient Egypt © 2006 The Learning Works

Mummies: Preparing for the Afterlife

The ancient Egyptians believed that for a person to continue to live after death, the body had to be protected from decay—it had to be mummified. They believed that the body had a soul, or ka, which was released from the body at the time of death. The ka did not stay peacefully in one place and needed to rest in the mummified body at night.

The process of mummification had two stages. First, bodies were embalmed before burial. The jackal-headed Anubis, the god of death and embalming, supervised the process of embalming. The brain and internal organs were removed. Then, the body was dressed and prepared according to strict rituals based largely on the Book of the Dead, a collection of ancient procedures and rituals. The process ended with the final procession to the burial tomb or pyramid.

Project Description

As the leading Egyptologist for the Ancient Egypt Museum, you attended a seminar on mummification in Cairo, Egypt. The first workshop was held in the Mummy Room of the Egyptian Museum. The displays of famous pharaohs left you speechless, and your jaw dropped open when you came face-to-face with the mummified head of Rameses II. You immediately call your staff and ask them to start making amazing mummy models for your museum's own Mummy Room.

Materials

papier mache materials
long balloons, newspaper, or foil
    for the frame
pre-made amulets (see page 50)
    from clay, cardboard amulets,
    or old costume jewelry
poster paints
varnish or commercial glaze, optional
scissors
clay (optional)

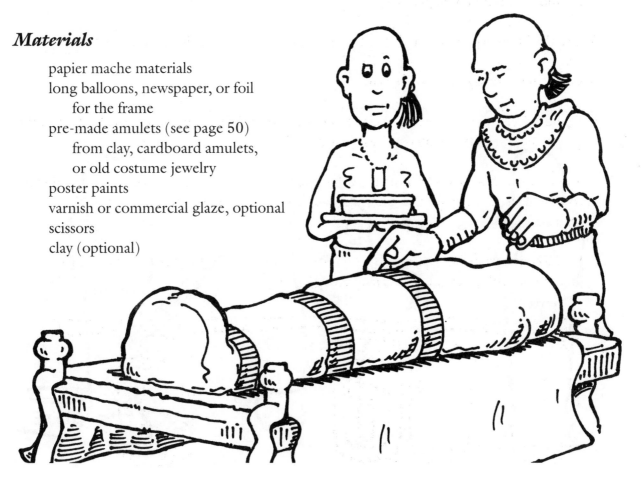

Mummies: Preparing for the Afterlife *(continued)*

Directions

Mummies can be made in any size using this technique and either increasing or decreasing the amount of materials. If you want to make a life-size mummy, you will need to use chicken wire, or something similar, for the frame. If you are going to make a sarcophagus for the mummy, coordinate the size of the mummy to the size of a common-sized box, like a shoe or boot box.

While you are making your mummy, visualize what happened during the mummification ceremony. Priests perform ceremonies; the brain is removed; the inner organs are removed and placed in canopic jars. Then the body cavity is stuffed with bundles of natron, covered with natron, placed on a tilted slab, and allowed to dry for about 40 days. The body is perfumed, repacked, and decorated; jewels and charms are tucked into twenty or so layers of linen strips which are wound around the body. At every layer, the bandages are painted with liquid resin that helps to glue the bandages together.

1. Choose either crumpled foil or a long balloon to make your form. Decide on the size of the mummy. Form the head and feet until it takes on a good "mummy" shape, by either compressing the foil in the appropriate places, or using rubber bands to constrict the balloon. Use masking tape to smooth down rough spots.

2. Papier mache the mummy form. Make amulets out of clay, cardboard, or paper, and place them in between layers of papier mache. Allow the mummy to dry thoroughly.

3. Seal the mummy by brushing on a coat of undiluted white glue. (optional)

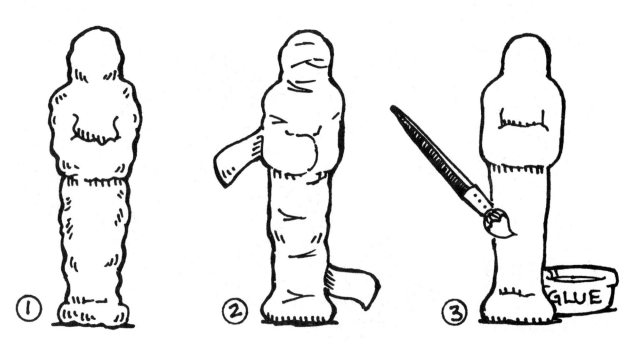

Mummies: Preparing for the Afterlife *(continued)*

4. Paint and decorate the wrapped mummy in a traditional way—a face mask, hieroglyphs, and pictures of gods and goddesses. When the paints have dried, the mummy can be glazed with varnish (optional). Let dry thoroughly.

   While you are decorating your mummy, visualize what happened during the mummification ceremony. The bound head is covered with a portrait mask so the ka can recognize it. Many masks were molded and painted, and sometimes they were made of gold. (See Mummy Masks activity on page 28.)

5. (Optional) Use clay to make a coffin for the mummy. Shape and paint it to look like a person. Be sure to make the coffin larger than the mummy. When the clay is dry, paint it in traditional ancient Egyptian style. Place the mummy inside the coffin.

   While you are making a coffin, visualize what really happened. The finished mummy was placed in a coffin or a series of nesting coffins. The coffins were painted inside and out with pictures of gods, goddesses, prayers, and magic spells; finally a splendid stone sarcophagus was made to hold the coffin.

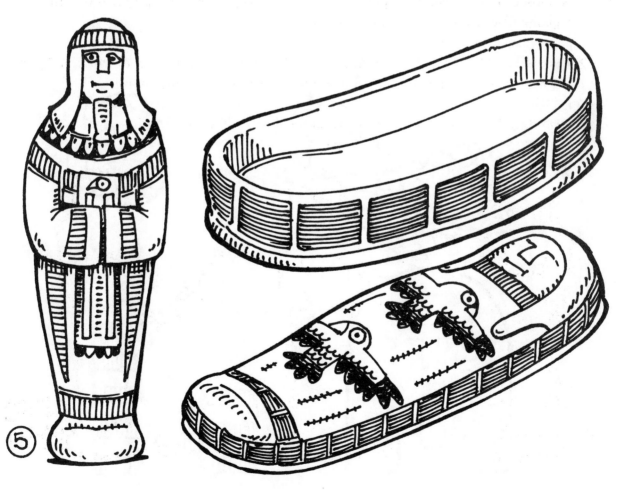

Ancient Egypt © 2006 The Learning Works

Mummy Masks

The Egyptians had to make sure the ka could recognize its own body. So after the mummy was wrapped in linen, a mask resembling the dead person was fitted over the head and shoulders. Funeral masks were made out of solid gold, wood, or cartonnage (plastered layers of fiber or papyrus). Wooden and cartonnage masks were painted or gilded with gold.

Project Description

The highlight of your tour of the Egyptian Museum in Cairo, Egypt, was getting a close look at the funeral mask of King Tutankhamun. Create a mummy mask of your own face for your Ancient Egypt Museum.

Materials

      poster board or cardboard
      heavy-duty foil, enough to cover a face with a four-inch
          border, or two layers of thinner foil for each mask
      masking tape
      papier mache materials
      scissors
      stapler
      paints
      marking pens

Mummy Masks *(continued)*

Directions

1. Cut the poster board or cardboard into the shape of a pharaoh's crown to replicate the sides of the mask.

2. Work with a partner. Place the sheet of foil over your partner's face. Gently mold the foil to conform to the features of the face, being careful to get a clear impression of the eyes, nose, and lips. Continue pressing the foil about two inches beyond the forehead. (You can make an impression of your own face if a partner is not available.)

3. Carefully remove the foil and check to see if the impression is clear; make corrections if necessary.

4. Papier mache the foil mask with a layer of newspaper. The mask is very delicate at this point so soak the newspaper until it is saturated with paste before placing it very gently on the foil. Be patient while this dries—a couple of hours or overnight. If part of the mask becomes indented, gently push it back into place from inside the mask.

5. Apply three or four more layers of papier mache to the mask.

6. When the mask is dry, carefully staple or tape it to the poster board crown.

7. Use masking tape to create a smooth transition between the foil and poster board crown.

8. (Optional) Cover the foil and the poster board with another thin layer of papier mache.

9. Paint your mask in the style of an ancient Egyptian death mask.

Canopic Jars

During the embalming part of mummification, internal organs were removed from the body, dried in salts, individually wrapped in linen, and placed in canopic jars. The lids of the canopic jars represented the four sons of the god Horus. They protected the contents of these jars.

The intestines went into the jar with the hawk head (Qebehsenuf); the stomach went into the jar with the jackal head (Duamutefla); the lungs went into the jar with the baboon head (Hapi); and the liver went into the jar with the human head (Imseti).

The two major organs that were left out of canopic jars were the heart and the brain. The Egyptians thought that the brain was useless so they dragged the brain out of the body through the nose with a metal hook and threw it away. The heart was usually left in the body.

Project Description

The curator of a famous ancient Egyptian museum was holding a special exhibition on funerary objects. The scientists entered the canopic jar room which was full of jars representing the various ancient Egyptian kingdoms. The jars that caught your attention were the ones made after the Nineteenth Dynasty—with lids in the form of one of the four children of Horus. These are the ones that you want to replicate for your museum, and you immediately call your artists to begin work on them.

Materials

> foil
> baby food jars, yogurt containers,
>   or similar containers
> masking tape
> papier mache materials
> permanent marking pens
> paints
> brushes

Canopic Jars *(continued)*

Directions

1. Choose one of the four styles of canopic jars (or choose all four) and make a drawing of what you want it to look like.

2. Create the head of the god out of foil following the directions on page 15. The foil will be attached to the lid of the jar or container, so make sure it fits those dimensions.

3. Tape the foil god to the container's lid.

4. Tape the lid to the jar or container. The canopic jar will have a smooth effect but will not be able to open; if you want it to open, papier mache each piece separately.

5. Completely cover the jar or container with papier mache. Use the papier mache to smooth out places that are bumpy or loose. Use paper towels or tissue paper for the last layer.

6. When the canopic jar is completely dry, use marking pens or paint to decorate it with appropriate designs and hieroglyphs.

Ancient Egypt © 2006 The Learning Works

An Ancient Sarcophagus

A sarcophagus is a large coffin made of stone or gold. They were expensive to make, so usually only pharaohs and queens, priests, and other important people were buried in them. A sarcophagus offered more protection for the mummy, and like the inner coffin, it was either shaped like a rectangular box or like a human.

Project Description

You and the expedition ease your way along the dark and narrow passageway. As you round the corner you spot the pharaoh's burial chamber with its doors protected by a sealed rope. The rope is removed, you enter the chamber, and there before your eyes is the famous sarcophagus. It is gold with four goddesses carved in high relief on the corners. Sparking jewels are set in patterns on the lid. You begin making drawings so you can replicate this sarcophagus for your own museum.

Materials

    shoe box or box slightly larger than a mummy
        that you would like to use for the sarcophagus
        (for a life-sized mummy, an appliance box
        can be used)
    papier mache materials
    marking pens
    tempera paints
    old jewelry, rhine-
        stones, glitter,
        or other deco-
        rative materials
    gold paint
    brushes
    white glue

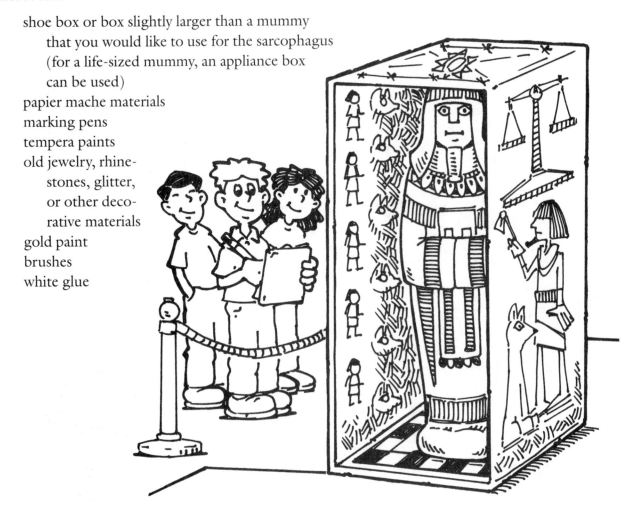

An Ancient Sarcophagus *(continued)*

Directions

These directions are for making a rectangular sarcophagus.

1. Use several layers of papier mache on both the lid and the bottom of the box that you have chosen for the sarcophagus. Use brown paper towels, or white paper, depending on the effect that you want. If you want the sarcophagus to open, papier mache the lid and the bottom separately.

2. Allow to dry thoroughly.

3. Brush on diluted white glue to act as a varnish, and let dry.

4. Paint gold and let it dry.

5. Add hieroglyphs and Egyptian drawings with marking pens or paint.

6. Decorate with jewels, beads, glitter, gold foil, and other decorative items.

Funerary Boat Model

The Nile River was the main travel route in ancient Egypt, and all the cities and towns were easily accessible by boat. Small boats, like fishing boats, were made from bundles of papyrus stalks lashed together with ropes. The larger boats were usually built of wood. The pharaohs prided themselves on their pleasure boats with multiple decks containing cabins, kitchens, dining rooms, and lounges.

Elaborate funerary boats were very important to the ancient Egyptians because these boats took the pharaohs to their tombs. According to their beliefs, the soul of the dead accompanied the sun on its eternal journey in the heavens around the world. Therefore a boat—or at least a model of a boat—was included in every tomb. In Tutankhamun's tomb there were thirty-five boats. The most famous boats are the two discovered in 1955 next to the great pyramid at Giza, although their exact purpose is still in dispute.

Project Description

You leave the site of the museum that houses the famous boats found at Giza and you find yourself imagining that you are working in one of the pharaoh's workshops—a special one that is creating the funerary boat for his final trip on the Nile before he is buried in his tomb. You are excited because you have come up with some ideas that will make this boat unique but still follow the basic designs of the ancient Egyptians. Make a drawing of your plan, and then construct a model of it to be displayed in the Ancient Egypt Museum.

Funerary Boat Model *(continued)*

Guidelines for making a funerary boat

Include a man who acts as lookout, slave rowers, a drummer who sets the pace for the rowers, a pilot to steer the rudder, a canopy, the dead pharaoh under the canopy, a priest, and various funerary objects like jars and boxes. Decorate the boat with drawings of lotus flowers, gods, and other symbolic designs. Paint it so some of its parts resemble gold or other precious metals.

Materials

> aluminum foil
> masking tape
> newspaper and white glue for papier mache
> bright acrylic paints
> gold paint
> permanent marking pens

Directions

1. Create the boat, people, and funeral objects out of aluminum foil. Follow the directions on page 15.

2. Flatten the foil on the bottom of the boat so it will sit upright on a table.

3. Put a thin layer of papier mache over the masking tape to create a smoother finish.

4. When the boat is completely dry, paint it and the figures. Add details with the permanent marking pens and gold paint.

Egyptian Pyramids

Egyptian pyramids are among the largest man-made structures ever conceived, and they are one of the enduring symbols of ancient Egypt. Approximately ninety pyramid structures of various sizes and in various states of preservation exist today. Each pyramid required careful planning, from choosing the site to hiring architects, builders, painters, carvers, and numerous craft people.

The first tombs were flat-roofed buildings called mastabas. They were used as burial chambers before pyramids were constructed. Over time, they evolved into the pyramids that we are familiar with today. Later on, the Egyptians decided to stop making pyramids and, instead, carved their pharaohs' tombs into the sides of cliffs.

Project Description

Your tour guide takes you out early in the morning to see the great Giza necropolis (a Greek word meaning "city of the dead"). He explains that Giza was chosen by King Khufu and his successors as the site of their pyramids. The site also contains funerary boats, the Sphinx, other royal pyramids, and private tombs. As the sun rises over the pyramids, you begin planning a model of the necropolis that can be placed in your Ancient Egypt Museum.

Guidelines for building a model of the Giza necropolis

1. Include several required components in your model—the Nile River, the Great Pyramid of Khufu, the Pyramid of Khafre, the Pyramid of Menkaure, and the Sphinx.

2. Optional components of the model could include one or more mastabas, the Queen's Pyramids, cemeteries, one or more causeways, Sphinx Temple, a funeral barge, a typical royal family and professional mourners, the pharaoh, and possessions ready to be placed in the pyramid.

Egyptian Pyramids *(continued)*

Materials

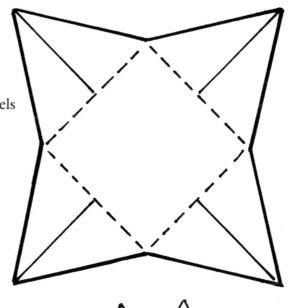

    a piece of plywood or heavy cardboard,
        for the base of the model
    poster board or cardboard
    sand or papier mache using brown paper towels
    glue
    scissors
    masking tape
    tempera paints or markers
    modeling compound for miniature
        components of model

Directions

1. If the model of the necropolis will be built in sections—or by groups of students—standardize the dimensions so the sections fit together.

2. Make a diagram of the model.

3. Cut the base to fit the dimensions of your model.

4. Cover the base with white glue. Sprinkle sand over the glue and let dry thoroughly. You can also use several layers of brown paper towel papier mache to cover the base to achieve a sandy look.

5. Build the pyramids from cardboard. Enlarge the pattern and use it as a guide.

6. Use tape and glue to assemble the different structures.

7. Create small items, like the possessions to be buried with the pharaoh, out of a modeling compound.

8. Decorate the model with paints, markers, or other items to make it look authentic.

Egyptian Columns

As priests became more powerful and religious ideas were firmly established, tombs became a part of great temples. Usually a temple was built in front of rugged sandstone cliffs. The tomb section was constructed deep into the cliff and included great columned halls, pylons, obelisks, and statues. Over thirty types of Egyptian columns have been identified. Column shafts were often decorated with colorful depictions in painted, carved relief. They are some of the most interesting architectural elements in Egyptian structures.

Palm Columns

These columns have a palm tree motif, representing the eight palm fronds on a palm tree.

Lotus Columns

The lotus column has ribbed shafts representing the stems of the lotus, and capitals (top of the column) in the form of either a closed bud or an open lotus flower.

Papyrus Columns

Some papyrus columns have circular shafts representing a single plant, while others have ribbed shafts that represent a plant with multiple stems. The capitals represent either closed buds or an open, bell-shaped form.

Egyptian Columns *(continued)*

Project Description

A hypostyle is any building or space resting on rows of pillars or columns. The most spectacular is the great Hypostyle Hall in the Karnak Temple of Amen-Re in Luxor. Some of the columns are 69 feet high and have open papyrus capitals. Other columns—122 of them—are 43 feet high and have closed papyrus-bud capitals. Design a hypostyle fit for a pharaoh; then make plans and drawings for the hypostyle. Make a model of one of the columns out of plaster of paris. Display both the column and your hypostyle plans in your museum.

Materials

> drawing paper
> plaster of paris
> disposable mixing container like a paper paint bucket
> mixing sticks
> water
> paper towel tube or cardboard to make a tube
> > (mold for tall, narrow column)
> carving tools such as chisels, dull kitchen knives,
> > nails wrapped in masking tape, old dental tools,
> > pointed nut crackers, nail file
> paints or permanent marking pens
> paper towels

Ancient Egypt © 2006 The Learning Works

Egyptian Columns *(continued)*

Directions

1. Choose the type of column you want to make. Make a pattern for the design that you will carve into the hardened plaster.

2. Mix plaster of paris according to the package directions.

3. When it is the right consistency—like sour cream—pour it into the tubular mold. Tap the bottom of the mold on a flat surface to release any trapped air.

4. The plaster will harden in just a few minutes. When the block is ready, peel the mold away, and discard the pieces.

5. You'll notice that the plaster may be warm. The plaster will be soft, so working with the column is easy at this stage.

6. Use a pencil to sketch a basic outline of your design on the column. Begin carving. Blowing the plaster dust will make your work area messy. Clean up your work area frequently with damp paper towels.

7. Be careful in cleaning up because plaster can clog sink drains. Clean your hands by wiping the plaster on a rag or paper towels, and then rinse in a bucket of water.

Royal Jewelry

Jewelry was worn by both men and women as a decoration or as a status symbol. Special pieces were believed to bring good luck or keep evil spirits away from the wearer. Crafts people created bracelets, earrings, necklaces, collars, and rings from gold, semi-precious stones, glass, and colorful beads.

Project Description

You are working in the jewelry workshop in ancient Giza preparing for the burial of a pharaoh. You must design a very special piece of jewelry that will be worn by the mummy. You draw upon your great knowledge of Egyptian culture to create a piece of jewelry fit for a pharaoh—and fit for display in the Ancient Egypt Museum thousands of years later.

Royal Jewelry *(continued)*

Option One: Necklace or Collar

Materials

> one of the designs from this page, one from
>> your research, or an original design
> cardboard
> scissors
> papier mache materials
> white paper, like paper towels or tissue
> white paint
> gold paint
> glitter, rhinestones, beads, foil,
>> old costume jewelry, etc.
> hole punch
> cording, thread, or yarn

Directions

1. Copy the outside shape of your design onto a piece of cardboard. Cut out the shape.

2. Apply a thin layer of papier mache over the cardboard. Finish with a layer of white paper. Allow to dry thoroughly.

3. Paint it white and let it dry.

4. Very lightly pencil in the design that you are using for your piece of jewelry. Then apply gold paint and the other decorative objects. Use permanent marking pens to add details.

5. Punch holes in each end of the necklace or collar. Tie on cording, thread, or yarn.

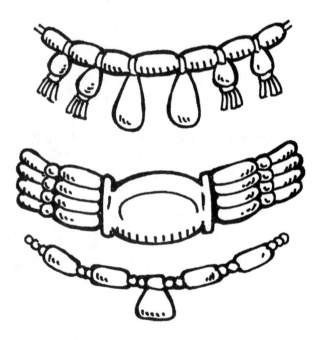

Royal Jewelry *(continued)*

Option Two: Beaded Jewelry

Materials

>   paper and marking pens to create a design for a beaded piece
>   of jewelry
>   sculpting clay that does not need firing
>   skewer or large paper clip
>   paints
>   marking pens
>   plastic knife
>   stringing material like string or thin cord

Directions

1. Prepare the design of the piece of jewelry that you will make.

2. To make a round bead, pinch off a small amount of clay and roll it between your palms into a ball shape. If the bead is lopsided, you can gently press it into shape. If you want a different shape, try rolling it on the table or carving out bits of the clay. Another technique is to roll the clay into a worm shape and slice it with a plastic knife into the lengths that you want.

3. When each bead is finished, make the stringing hole by piercing it with a skewer or opened paper clip.

4. When the clay has hardened, paint the beads in traditional Egyptian colors and designs.

5. When the beads are dry, string them with thin cord or string.

Scarab Jewelry Box

One of the most important creatures in ancient Egypt was the scarab or dung beetle. The ancient Egyptians observed the beetle as it collected animal dung, rolled it into a ball, and pushed it into a hole in the ground where it laid its eggs. Soon, the birth of another generation of beetles was observed. This reminded the Egyptians of the sun as it made its way across the sky, descended into the underworld each night, and was reborn the next morning. Often, the beetle is associated with the sun god Ra.

Scarab jewelry, amulets, containers, and other decorative items were made in a wide variety of materials such as lapis lazuli, basalt, limestone, turquoise, colored glass, and alabaster. Pottery scarabs were also produced, carved when dry, and colored with glazes.

Project Description

As the pharaoh's head jeweler, you are in charge of creating unique jewelry and the containers for storing the jewelry. The pharaoh has requested a special scarab box for his daughter's thirteenth birthday. Create one worthy of being viewed and admired by people centuries hence and recognized for its unique design and beauty.

Scarab Jewelry Box *(continued)*

Materials

    clay that doesn't require firing or baking
      (about 2 inches in diameter)
    sculpting tools like paper clips, pins, toothpicks
    unfinished box from a craft store, or a small gift box
    gold, turquoise, and blue paints
    glue
    black, red, and blue permanent marking pens
    piece of cardboard slightly larger than the scarab

Directions

1. Create the scarab out of the clay. The size should be slightly smaller than the lid of the box you are using. The typical Egyptian scarab is shaped like an egg cut in half with a flat underside.

2. Incise the lines that form the body with sculpting tools.

3. When the scarab is dry, paint it turquoise or blue. Outline the incised lines with black marking pen to make them stand out.

4. Cut out a piece of cardboard slightly larger than the scarab and paint it gold.

5. Glue the scarab onto the cardboard when it is dry.

6. Paint the box and box lid gold.

7. Heiroglyphs, symbols, or names were incised on the underside of the scarab. Since your scarab will be glued to the lid of the box, you might want to use marking pens to create the writing and drawings on the underside of the lid of the box.

8. Glue the cardboard with the scarab onto the lid of the box. Let it dry thoroughly.

9. Use marking pens to draw ancient Egyptian patterns and designs around the outside of the box.

A Queen's Portrait

Hatshepsut was probably the most extraordinary female ruler in ancient Egypt. She declared herself pharaoh, won the support of key officials, and ruled from 1503 to 1484 B.C. Because Egyptians saw kingship as a male privilege, she donned a false beard as a sign of authority. Carvings in her honor describe how she encouraged trade with eastern Mediterranean lands. Her greatest triumph was an expedition sent to Punt (perhaps present day Somalia). Ships returned loaded with sweet smelling resin, ivory, spices, leopard skins, medicines, aromatic trees, and live monkeys for private zoos.

Project Description

Many artists, both ancient and modern, create portraits of Queen Hatshepsut. Make a foil repousse of Hatshepsut and hang it in your museum.

Materials

heavy gauge aluminum foil, about 9 inches x 12 inches (store
   bought heavy duty foil will work but more care will be
   needed in transferring the design to the foil)
black poster board or card stock, several inches
   larger than the foil
stapler
newspapers
masking tape
blunt pencil, ball point pen, paint brush
   handle, craft sticks, or modeling tools
black India ink
paint brush
paper towels
permanent marking pens

Ancient Egypt © 2006 The Learning Works

A Queen's Portrait *(continued)*

Directions

1. Sketch a picture of Hatshepsut the same size as the foil.

2. Carefully fold back the edges of the foil about 1/2 inch for a finished look.

3. Tape the sketch to the aluminum foil to prevent it from moving.

4. Place a thick pad of newspaper on the work area. If newspaper isn't used, the lines in the repousse won't transfer.

5. Go over every line of the sketch to transfer it to the foil. Trace over all lines with a ball point pen or other blunt tool. Press down into the foil without going through it.

6. Refine the design by adding lines, dots, extra designs, and details directly to the foil.

7. Antique the repousse by brushing on black India ink and wiping off the desired amount. Or use permanent marking pens to create a colorful repousse.

8. Staple the repousse to a piece of black poster board or card stock.

Ancient Egypt © 2006 The Learning Works

Abu Simbel Poster Talk

Few pharaohs are associated with so many events and monumental building projects as Ramses the Great, or Ramses II. He became pharaoh when he was 20 and died in his 90th year, a respected king and statesman who oversaw one of the most prosperous eras in ancient Egypt.

The Battle of Kadesh was one of Ramses' first tests on the battlefield. It became famous in part because Ramses had the details of it recorded on several temples, including those at Abydos, Abu Simbel, and Karnak.

Not only is he known as one of Egypt's greatest warriors, but also as a peace-maker, and for the monuments he left behind like the religious temples built in Karnak, Luxor, Abu Simbel, and Abydos. Today Ramses the Great's mummy can be seen at the Egyptian Museum in Cairo, Egypt.

Project Description

The two temples at Abu Simbel are magnificent monuments. On the front of the Great Temple are four huge statues of the king, each 67 feet high. Also sculpted on the front are his mother, one of his wives, and eight of his 140 children. A temple is cut behind the statues approximately 200 feet into the hillside. When the Aswan Dam was constructed in the 1960s, it was clear that these unique monuments would be covered by the waters of Lake Nasser. An artificial cliff was built above the original site. During the salvage operation, the temples were dismantled and raised up to the artificial cliff and reassembled. Create an educational poster for your museum that highlights the history of Abu Simbel. Be prepared to use the poster in an informative talk to museum visitors.

Abu Simbel Poster Talk *(continued)*

Materials

poster board
research materials about Ramses II and Abu Simbel
paints or marking pens
pictures from magazines or the Internet
ruler

Guidelines for some topics to include on the poster

Ramses II
Abu Simbel
Reconstruction of Abu Simbel
The temples at Abu Simbel
Map
Ramses' cartouche and his mummy
Pictures, drawings, hieroglyphs

Directions

1. Research Ramses II and Abu Simbel. Make a sketch of what you will include in your poster.

2. Begin working on the poster by lightly drawing in the components.

3. Paint or use marking pens to complete the poster. Glue on pictures.

4. Prepare a short talk using the poster as a visual aid.

Amulets

Do you believe in good luck or in any object that you believe carries an aura of magic, or luck, with it? Ancient Egyptians believed so strongly in the healing and protective power of the amulet that they sought its protection not only during life, but also in the afterlife.

Amulets came in many forms. Some were taken from hieroglyphs; some looked like animals and other natural forms. They were made of gold, silver, gems, or wood, and were often combined with other jewelry.

Popular designs for amulets included the following:

Udjat: Hieroglyphic sign for "lasting good health, safety, and happiness" under the protection of Ra. It is often referred to as the "Eye of Horus."

Ankh: Hieroglyphic sign for everlasting life. It is one of the most ancient amulets, and one of Egypt's most powerful symbols.

Re (Ra): The solar disk, a sign of the sun god Re.

Tyet or Isis knot: Isis was the wife of Osiris, god of the underworld. She helped the dead reach the afterlife. This amulet provided magical protection for reaching the afterlife.

Scarab: One of several amulets dedicated to the Sun God Ra, and one of the most important of over thirty funerary amulets. The Scarab was a stylized depiction of the dung beetle, which ancient Egyptians used to illustrate life-giving powers.

Bes: An amulet that entertained children as well as protected them. Bes had a fearsome appearance which was designed to scare evil forces from the home, but he was kind and good-hearted in nature.

Amulets *(continued)*

Project Description

During your research, you become fascinated with ancient Egyptian amulets, especially those found by Egyptologists working at the Giza necropolis. There are about fifty or sixty of them, and they are made of carved stone, ivory, bronze, and faience. Your Ancient Egypt Museum needs some amulets, too, to represent those found wrapped in mummies, buried with mummies in fancy coffins, and inscribed on walls and tombs. Make an amulet from clay that replicates an Egyptian amulet or make one of your own design but following traditional Egyptian design.

Materials

> modeling clay that doesn't require firing
> roller or brayer
> carving tools like a plastic knife, nail, or toothpick
> paints
> amulet patterns

Directions

1. Make a sketch of the amulet that you want to make.

2. Roll out a ball of clay with a roller or brayer.

3. Use a carving tool to cut out the amulet.

4. When it is dry, it can be painted in bright colors.

Ancient Egypt © 2006 The Learning Works

Wall Mural

The ancient Egyptians decorated the walls of their palaces, temples, and tombs with brightly painted murals. The scenes usually depicted everyday life, including parties, farming practices, pottery making, fishing, and all sorts of animals and fish. The murals also portrayed religious processions, embalming procedures, and activities of gods and goddesses. These brightly-colored murals give a unique insight into ancient Egyptian life.

Wall Mural *(continued)*

Project Description

As your expedition reached the long corridor leading to the burial chamber, you heard people gasp in amazement. The corridor walls were painted from floor to ceiling with pictures of the pharaoh in everyday life, gods and goddesses, hieroglyphs, and inscriptions. The gods appeared to be protecting the deceased on his dangerous journey to the underworld. Create a mural for your museum that would be appropriate for a pharaoh's burial chamber or palace.

Egyptian art had strict conventions for representing the human body:

Gods and other important figures are larger in size than everyone else in the scene.

Many Egyptian gods had the body of a person but the head of an animal.

The head of a person is represented from a side view—a profile. The person's eye stares out from the side of the head.

The legs of a person are drawn in profile.

The torso is turned fully to the front.

Both feet appear flat on the ground, even in walking figures.

Most men are shown in pleated kilts; most women wear linen dresses.

Most mural colors were limited to black, blue, red, white, green, and yellow.

Wall Mural *(continued)*

The ancient Egyptians believed that gods and goddesses controlled the forces of nature and all things including birth and death and the seasons. Here are a few of the gods and goddesses represented in murals:

Bastet is represented by a woman with a cat's head.

Horus is represented by a falcon.

Hathor held the sun between her horns.

Isis is shown with cow's horns and the solar disk.

Osiris wears the White Crown of Upper Egypt and holds a flail and crook.

Anubis is represented by a man with a dog or jackal's head.

Bastet | Horus

 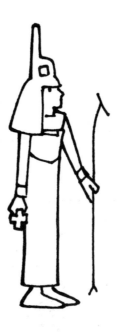  

Hathor | Isis | Osiris | Anubis

Ancient Egypt © 2006 The Learning Works

Wall Mural *(continued)*

Materials

white art paper or brown wrapping paper,
36 inches to 46 inches wide
paints and brushes
research materials, if necessary
black marking pens
gold paint
stapler or tape

Directions

The Egyptians used a technique called bas-relief, or low relief, to produce their murals on walls. They actually carved the figures on the wall allowing them to project out slightly from the stone wall. You can make a bas-relief by mixing plaster of paris, pouring it into a mold, and carving on it when it is dry. However, a painted mural will allow more flexibility in working with other students, and will create a larger, more dramatic, piece of art.

1. Make a class plan for the mural. Discuss how much space each student will need; whether or not the mural will be a coordinated group mural or many independent scenes; and what the mural will portray.

2. Staple or tape the mural paper on a flat surface in the classroom.

3. Work independently or with a partner to make a preliminary sketch of the mural. Try to include at least one god in your plans.

4. Using a pencil, lightly draw in figures, hieroglyphs, and cartouches on the mural paper.

5. Paint the figures and use a black marking pen to finish the hieroglyphs and cartouches.

6. Add gold paint where appropriate.

     Ancient Egypt © 2006 The Learning Works

Ancient Egyptian Harp

Beautifully decorated Egyptian harps were an important component of ancient religious ceremonies, banquets, and social gatherings. Other instruments were lutes, drums, cymbals, bells, tambourines, flutes, and trumpets.

Harps were usually made in one of two ways—a small portable or shoulder harp, or a much larger arched harp. Both were plucked rather than bowed. The portable harp was made out of wood and had eight to twelve strings made from animal gut. This type of harp was often decorated with expensive materials like silver, gold, and lapis lazuli, and covered with flowery or geometrical ornamentations. In one picture on a tomb, a harp is shown with a jaguar's skin, an instrument for rich people.

Project Description

You have just toured the tomb of an 18th Dynasty prince. One of the murals in the tomb showed part of a banquet scene with a strolling lute player and two other musicians playing harps. The mural is supposed to show the pleasant scenes of the afterlife with the female musicians playing for the soul of the deceased throughout eternity. You notice that the portable harp is made out of gold and alabaster and a dark, rich wood. It is so beautiful that you begin plans to make a reproduction of this harp for the Ancient Egypt Museum.

Ancient Egyptian Harp *(continued)*

Materials

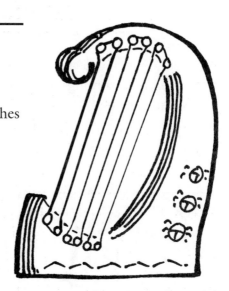

pattern of your harp design
4 pieces of cardboard or posterboard, about 15 x 15 inches
extra cardboard to add stability to the base
stapler or glue
paints in gold and a variety of bright colors
assorted rubber bands
scissors
hole punch
brads

Directions

1. Draw a pattern for the portable harp. Be creative but follow ancient Egyptian artistic techniques. Include ideas for how it will be painted.

2. Make four tracings of the pattern onto the cardboard and cut out the four pieces.

3. Measure and mark the location of holes for the harp strings on one piece and punch the holes. Lay the punched piece on each of the remaining pieces, mark the location of the holes, and punch them. Make six holes on the top and six on the bottom.

4. Glue or staple all four pieces together, keeping the holes aligned. If you use glue, let it dry thorougly.

5. Paint and decorate the harp with elaborate yet traditional designs.

6. Place a brad in each of the twleve holes.

7. Wrap a rubber band around two adjacent brads on the top of the harp, then stretch the rubber band across the harp and wrap it around the two corresponding brads on the bottom, making two "strings." Repeat for the remaining pairs of brads. Use thicker or longer rubber bands for the low notes, thinner or shorter rubber bands for the high notes. Adjust the tension of the rubber bands so that the notes sound good together.

Ancient Egypt © 2006 The Learning Works

Cloisonné Tiles

Egyptian designs reflect natural plant or animal forms found in the environment. Some designs found on vases, paintings, and jewelry are drawn from the shapes of the lotus plant, papyrus, palm, and scarab. The designs are made up of different lines and marks which are repeated throughout the art work.

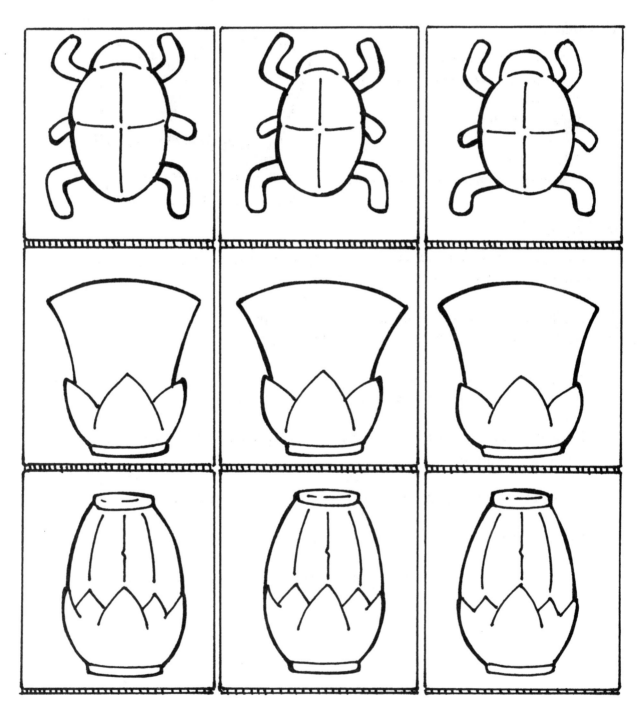

Ancient Egypt © 2006 The Learning Works

Cloisonné Tiles *(continued)*

Project Description

The director of the Ancient Egypt Museum, after consulting with leading Egyptian designers, asked the museum staff to create a series of cloisonné tiles based on patterns used by ancient Egyptian artisans. Research designs and patterns, create the tiles, and mount them for display.

Materials

    heavy duty foil, about 5 x 5 inches
    cardboard squares, about 4 x 4 inches
    white glue
    string (optional)
    scissors
    masking tape
    permanent marking pens in bright colors

Directions

1. Use a pencil to outline your design on the piece of cardboard. It is easier to work with simple lines and patterns.

2. Outline the pattern with white glue. Let it dry thoroughly. If you make another outline on top of the dried glue, let that dry thoroughly, also.

3. An optional design technique is to place string on top of the glue before it dries. It is easier to work with small lengths of string, cut to fit the pattern.

4. Place the piece of foil over the cardboard, turn over, and tape down the edges of foil to the back of the cardboard.

5. On the front, use your fingers to press the foil down into the low areas.

6. Color in the low areas with permanent marking pens.

7. Glue or tape the finished tile to a piece of matte board or construction paper.

Ancient Egypt © 2006 The Learning Works

Vessel Etching

The exquisite Egyptian vessels that we see in museums are made out of gold, carved out of hard stone, or formed from glass, and only the richest could afford them. Ordinary people used clay vessels for drinking, cooking, eating, and carrying liquids.

Ancient Egyptian artisans experimented with many different kinds of rock in the manufacture of vessels including obsidian, alabaster, gold, and white limestone. They also used gemstones like carnelian, lapis lazuli, and amethyst. They also tried a number of techniques to improve the look of their pottery. Decorations were incised, painted, or stuck on. Pigments were applied to the clay. Faience—a mixture of blue or greenish quartzite particles and alkaline—was used. Flower designs, like papyrus and lotus plants, were used for decorations. Animals like hippos, ostriches, gazelles, crocodiles, flamingos, fish, iguanas, turtles, lions, and ibis were added as decorations, too.

Ancient Egypt © 2006 The Learning Works

Vessel Etching *(continued)*

Project Description

An etching is usually done on glass or metal plates by using a sharp tool to make the image. You have been given the challenge of creating a beautiful ancient Egyptian vessel etching by using the same method, only substituting paper for the glass or metal.

Materials

crayons of all colors
black crayons to fully cover the drawing paper
heavy white drawing paper 8½ x 11 or 9 x 12 inches
rulers
pencils
sharp objects such as a nail, cuticle stick, toothpicks,
    and some clay molding tools for scratching
    through the crayon.
newspaper
construction paper, larger than the drawing paper

Directions

1. Research ancient Egyptian vases and jars, and choose a design that you think will make an appealing etch.

2. Draw the outline of your vessel on the drawing paper and cut it out.

3. Place newspaper on your work surface.

4. Cover the vessel cutout with a thick layer of crayon. Choose colors that are authentic to the Egyptian vase. The entire paper vessel should be covered with color.

5. Cover the colors with a thick layer of black crayon, covering the whole paper vessel. Work carefully because the black crayon makes flakes.

6. Referring to your design, use a sharp object to scratch lines through the top layer to reveal the colored layers underneath.

7. Mount the etched paper vessel on contrasting colored construction paper.

Egyptian Shaduf Model

The Nile River was the center of Egyptian lives. It flooded in July, and the floodwaters carried rich soil that was deposited over fields. The Egyptians called this period the "inundation." After the inundation, farmers planted seeds.

Egyptians learned to save enough floodwater to last the whole year by cutting canals and ditches to store the water and carry it to their gardens, orchards, and vineyards. To lift the water from the canals they would use a *shaduf*—an irrigation tool originally developed in ancient Sumer. A *shaduf* is a large pole balanced on a crossbeam, a rope and bucket (or skin bag or reed basket) on one end and a heavy counterweight (made from clay or stone) at the other. Pulling on the rope lowers the bucket into the water source. The counterweight raises the bucket. The farmer would then carry the bucket to the field and water his plants. The *shaduf* is still in use in many parts of the world.

Project Description

On your travels in Lower Egypt along the Nile river, you spot several farmers using a *shaduf* to raise buckets of water. If the same buckets were lifted without the *shaduf*, the farmers would have to use the muscles of their backs, which would cause stress and possible injury. You want to illustrate the uniqueness of this ancient irrigation technique for your Ancient Egypt Museum and decide that the best way is to make a model of it.

　　　　　　　　　　　　　　　　　　Ancient Egypt © 2006 The Learning Works

Egyptian Shaduf Model *(continued)*

Materials

piece of plywood or heavy cardboard
one stick or dowel for the large pole
(choose sticks in proportion to the
size of the *shaduf* you will be making)
one stick or dowel for the crossbeam
two sticks to support the crossbeam
string
twine to simulate the rope
papier mache materials to make bucket
clay for the counterweight
clay to support the crossbeam
posterboard
paints
scissors
environmental items like rocks, sand, and plants
(actual items or clay models)

Optional

toy animals or make models of animals found along the Nile
wetlands such as lions, antelopes, deer, ibex, birds, fish,
crocodiles, hippopotami, and rhinoceroses

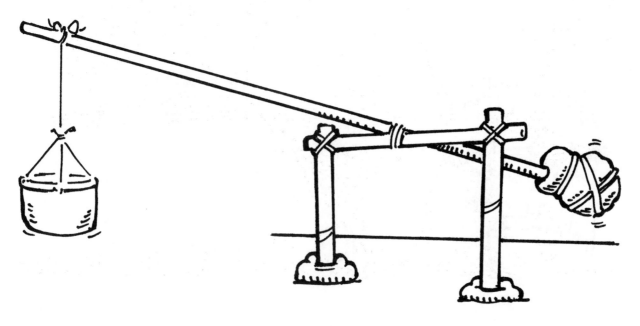

Ancient Egypt © 2006 The Learning Works

Egyptian Shaduf Model *(continued)*

Directions

1. Adhere two small mounds of clay to the piece of plywood or heavy cardboard about 5 inches apart or in the width that you will be making the crossbeam of the *shaduf.*

2. Put one stick upright in each of the mounds of clay.

3. Anchor one stick to the top of the upright crossbeam supports by tying with string at each end.

4. Attach an egg-shaped piece of clay to one end of the longer stick. This will be the counterweight. On the opposite end of the stick, tie a piece of twine or heavy string. Start with about 12 inches of twine and shorten if necessary.

5. At the end of the twine, attach the basket or bucket that you made out of papier mache or clay.

6. Experiment with the balance of the *shaduf.* When it seems in equilibrium, anchor the longer stick to the crossbeam with string.

7. Display the *shaduf* in a setting that shows how it was used by ancient Egyptians. For example, you can paint a piece of posterboard to look like water, sprinkle sand around the edges of the water, and add grasses, animals, and rocks for authenticity. Create a raised ledge or small cliff with clay or foil covered in masking tape and paint it. Finally, add the *shaduf* model to the scene.

Ancient Egypt © 2006 The Learning Works